The Cry *of the* Misfits *and the* Discarded

The Cry *of the* Misfits *and the* Discarded

ALIZA SNEED

THE CRY OF THE MISFITS AND THE DISCARDED
Copyright © 2015 by Aliza Sneed

ISBN: 978-0692606285

Author website: www.israelmyfriend.com

Interior and cover design by www.truenorthpublish.com

Printed in the United States of America. For worldwide distribution.

This book is dedicated to all those
who have felt the sting of rejection
and the pain of not fitting in.
Just as there was purpose and destiny
for each of the characters in these parables,
so there is hope for each of you.

Contents

Preface

Sitting on a boulder overlooking the beautiful Sea of Galilee, I noticed a spoon half buried in the soil a few feet away.

Suddenly it was as if the spoon had a voice with which he was bemoaning the fact that he had been discarded. Upon hearing all the details of his plight I carefully slipped down the embankment and retrieved the spoon from the dirt and debris that covered it. Just as I was holding the spoon in my hand, a stranger passed by.

"Are you OK?" he asked.

"If talking to a discarded spoon is OK, then I guess I'm fine," I said with a hearty laugh.

After showing him the spoon and sharing the story, the stranger informed me that something similar had happened in that area twenty years prior.

After that, I began going out each day with a pad and pen. As I passed a vacant lot, I saw many discarded items. Each seemed to be clamoring to tell their story, including an outdated computer, a palm branch that was lying in a mud puddle, along with a discarded fashion boot. As I sat down to write, I sensed an angelic presence, prompting me with what the Lord wanted me to say.

I later discovered that Hannah Hurnard who wrote *Hinds Feet on High Places* had at one time lived in that area. Little wonder that the urge to write had been so strong.

Hopefully these parables will bring a greater awareness of the Cry of the Misfits and Discarded people that surrounds us and that somehow we can reach out to them in a more compassionate way.

Aliza Sneed
November 2015

PARABLE *of the* DISCARDED SPOON

Chapter 1

"Come with me," said the little old woman. She took my arm and led me along the gravel path to a clearing that overlooked the Sea of Galilee. Although I was busy that day, I did not hesitate to go with her. Indeed, it was refreshing to take a break, especially since I had been glued to my computer for hours.

As we walked along the path, I saw many beautiful homes that looked like mansions, yet each was unique. However, they all had one thing in common—a colorful array of flowers, shrubbery, and clinging vines.

After reaching our destination, my eyes were captivated by the beauty of the rolling hillside as it stretched out its loving arms to embrace the placid sea. In the distance, a jagged row of mountains added to the grandeur of this panoramic view. Near the water's edge, cars and buses looked like ants scurrying along on a ribbon of black pavement.

As I stood there quietly absorbing this magnificent sight, the little old woman tugged at my arm. I thought she wanted to point out some unique place I had overlooked or draw my attention to the cooing of a dove on a nearby branch. Instead she began telling me an unusual story of love and compassion.

"Like you," she said, "I came here a few days ago to absorb the beauty of God's creation. I seated myself on one of the nearby boulders when suddenly I heard a mournful cry coming from over there," she said as she pointed to a steep slope several feet away. "As I looked more closely," she continued, "I discovered that the voice was that of a half-buried spoon!"

"I never thought I would end up like this," the spoon said with a heavy sigh.

"Oh, you poor spoon. Why would anyone want to discard you?" the old woman said with heartfelt sympathy.

"Things weren't always like this," replied the spoon, as if needing to apologize for the dirt that covered its once shiny surface. "When I was first made, I had no scrapes or scratches like you see now. Neither was any dirt found on me. In fact, I came from a family that had four shiny teaspoons, plus some cousins called forks. However, I proudly wore the title of a tablespoon!

"I alone had the pleasure of serving food to the family with whom we lived. The part I liked best was serving them on Shabbat, and all the other Biblical Feasts that they celebrated.

"For the first couple of years all went well, that is, until the fatal day when there came an unexpected knock on the door. Although I could not see the police officer," said the spoon as it continued its tragic story, "I knew something terrible must have happened.

'It can't be! It can't be,' the mother screamed hysterically as the officer informed her that her husband died in a car accident.

'I'm sorry,' said the police officer. 'Both your husband and the other driver were killed instantly when the two cars collided.'

"After that tragedy, no laughter filled the air and no meals were prepared except those brought in by neighbors and friends. I grieved over the death of this loving father as did the others. However, my deepest concern was for their little boy who was only eight years old. He wouldn't play or laugh or even talk to anyone. His eyes revealed the anger and sadness of his soul. Slowly he changed, becoming stubborn and rebellious.

"One day, after eating lunch, the boy's mom asked him to place his dirty dishes in the sink. In defiance he grabbed me up and ran out the door. When he came to this spot, he began unleashing his pent up anger by jabbing me into the dirt time after time, whereby the sharp rocks scratched my gleaming surface.

"Within a few minutes, his mother called him to come inside. With one last blow, he stabbed me into the ground so hard that my stem bent in this awkward way. Early the next morning a moving van pulled up in front of the house, and I never saw the family again," mourned the spoon.

"That," the old woman told me, "is what the spoon shared with me the day I found it."

"Did you ask the spoon how long ago these things happened?" I inquired.

"I think twelve years ago or more."

"Then what happened? Did you leave it in the dirt?" I asked.

"Of course not!"

"I thought you said the spoon was down that steep hill."

"It was, but I didn't let that stop me!" said the feisty old woman. "After slowly and carefully inching my way down to where the spoon was laying, I gently picked it up and cradling it in my hand, I said, 'Precious spoon, I'll take you home with me and give you a bath. You will be okay.'

'No,' the spoon protested, 'leave me here. My purpose on earth has ended.'

'Not! You will be my treasured possession for as long as I live, I said reassuringly.

"True to my word, I took the spoon home with me and cleaned it up," she added. "At first the other spoons were jealous. However, as time went by, they learned to love the spoon as much as I did," the old woman said with a smile.

After she finished her story, I walked with her back to her apartment. As we parted company, I thanked her for sharing this most unusual story.

Chapter 2

Several years later, I returned to Israel. I was eager to find the old woman and tell her what a profound impact the story of the discarded spoon had made on my life. Much to my sorrow, I found that she had recently gone home to be with her Creator.

I visited her friends, to inquire as to what had become of her beloved spoon. They informed me that all of her belongings, including the spoon, had been given to a charitable organization called Helping Hands Ministry.

After getting the address of the organization, I went there with the hope of finding the spoon. Most of the woman's belongings were still there except for the bent spoon; it was nowhere in sight.

When I asked the woman at the counter about the spoon her eyes lit up. "I know exactly the spoon you are talking about," she said with excitement.

"When the woman's things were first brought in, I helped sort through them. When I came across that spoon I was ready to throw it away, thinking surely no one will want an old scratched spoon like that. Just as I was about to toss it in the trash, a young couple came over to where I had been sorting the items.

"'I'm sorry, customers are not allowed in this part of the store,' I said politely.

"'You don't understand. My new bride and I are looking for a certain spoon that belonged to the old woman who recently passed away. We were told that her possessions were given to this store. We've come here to look for the spoon.'

"'Could this possibly be the spoon you are referring to?'" I asked, holding up the bent spoon.

"'Yes it is!' the young man said with a big smile. Quickly he grabbed the spoon from my hand and held it up for his bride to see. 'Beth,' he said. 'I've found it! I found the spoon I discarded. See, it's bent from the harsh treatment I gave it.' His wife seemed as delighted about the discovery as he was."

"So did the young man and his wife take the spoon home with them?" I asked inquisitively.

"They certainly did!" the store clerk said with a chuckle.

"Do you by chance know where this young couple lives? I would like to make some inquiries about this unusual spoon."

"Why? What has sparked your interest?" the woman asked.

"I was a friend of the old woman. In fact, I lived near her when she first found the spoon. I'm actually hoping to purchase it as a keepsake of our friendship."

"You are welcome to try," the woman said as she handed me the address of the couple. "But I doubt they will part with the spoon."

After thanking the woman for her help, I drove to the young couple's house.

When they answered the door, I introduced myself and explained my interest in the spoon. The couple invited me in. As we sipped coffee together, the young man filled me in on the details of what happened after he left the spoon in the dirt.

"I continued to be angry about the death of my dad," he said rather apologetically. "Nothing anyone could say or do could change my feelings.

"About a year later, my mom met a very nice man who wanted to marry her. Although she loved him, she refused to marry him for fear it would upset me. She was right. It would have infuriated me as I felt no one could take my dad's place.

"After mom broke up with this man, he married someone else. Even though my mom grieved, she said she never regretted her decision, as my happiness was more important than her own.

"It wasn't long after this that the bills began to pile up. Mom had to get a job working in a shoe factory. She put in long hours with only a small amount of pay, yet she never complained. After school one day, I was at home alone. Knowing my mom would not be home for several hours, I reheated a slice of pizza and sat down in the living room to watch television.

"As I was flipping through the stations, the news channel was reporting a fire. I heard the reporter say there had been a boiler explosion at one of the local factories. Five people were killed and fifteen injured.

"I picked up the TV remote to change the channel. But just as I did, the name of the factory flashed on the screen. In shock, I saw it was the shoe factory where my mom worked. The memory of my dad's death instantly flashed through my mind. I quickly threw down the remote to call mom's cell phone, but there was no answer.

"I cried out to God to spare my mom's life. At that point I had no idea if there really was a God. But since mom believed in Him, I would at least ask for help in case he was there. Somewhere deep inside of me, I heard a voice say, 'It will be okay my son.' At that moment, a deep peace settled over me.

"For the next two hours, I stayed glued to the television for any new developments. Suddenly, I saw my mom on the screen. Her clothes were partially burned, and her face was blackened by the smoke. She appeared to be pulling something from the burning building.

"'Mom let it go,' I yelled at the television. 'Let it go! The building is about to collapse. Run for your life.'

"Just as I said that, part of the roof fell and knocked her to the ground. As the firefighter rushed to rescue her, she still clung tightly to the object she had been dragging. Then I saw this was not an object at all, but rather one of her co-workers.

"When they announced the name of the hospital she and the others were being taken to, I asked a neighbor to take me to her. Mom was in the intensive care unit when I arrived, for she had slipped into a coma. The doctor said she had bravely saved the life of her co-worker but she herself had only a 50/50 chance of surviving.

"In spite of the negative report, the comforting words, 'It will be okay, my son' kept coming back to me. 'No, it won't,' another voice clamored loudly. 'Your mom is going to die just like your dad did.' For the next two hours, I battled to silence the sinister voice and to hold tightly to the promise of hope.

"During this time, Dan, the man whom my mom once loved, came to the hospital. He told me he had rushed there as soon as he heard the news. He asked if I would like to go with him to the chapel to pray.

"I was glad to go with him, as I felt perhaps this would silence the disparaging voice in my head. As we prayed, the peace I felt in the beginning filled my heart. With deep assurance, I knew my mom would recover.

"Later that afternoon, Dan and I had a long talk. I wished that I had not selfishly opposed him marrying my mom. Indeed he was a very compassionate, caring person. Finally, I braved the conversation enough to inquire about his wife.

"I'm not married," he replied.

"In response to my quizzical look he said, 'I know I was not truthful. I let everyone think I was getting married when I left town. I even let your mom think that. I couldn't bear staying here and seeing her torn between her love for you and her love for me. So I just told her I had found someone else, when I knew in my heart I could never find anyone that could take your mom's place in my life.'

"Over the next few days, mom's life continued to hang in the balance. On the third day, she awoke from the coma. She smiled when she saw me standing next to her bed. When I told her that Dan had come to the hospital to see her, tears filled her eyes. Then I told her he had not gotten married after all.

"I wish you could have seen the expression on her face when Dan walked in the room. Had it not been for the IV's in her arm and the cast on her leg, I think mom would have jumped out of bed to greet him. I firmly believe that his coming back into her life contributed to her miraculous recovery.

"As soon as mom was released from the hospital, she and Dan were married. At Dan's insistence, I was the best man at the wedding. The truth is, he is the best man! Or should I say, the best dad I could ever have.

"In fact, it was Dan who introduced me to Beth. She and I knew from the moment we met that we were destined to marry. Had I not laid aside my anger and self-centeredness and recognized Dan for who he really is, Beth and I might never have met.

"Actually, it was Beth that encouraged me to search for the spoon," the young man said as he reached over and lovingly took her hand. "Having come from a Jewish background, she was taught to look at animals and even objects as if they had feelings. They believe that in teaching this to their children, they will be more sensitive to people.

"So when I told her about the spoon and how I had damaged it in a fit of rage, she suggested that we come here on our honeymoon and look for it.

"We first went to the spot where I had originally discarded it. Although we knew the odds of finding it was next to impossible, we began checking through the debris. Just as we were about to give up, an old man from across the street asked what we were looking for. He told us that an old woman had found the spoon several years ago and took it home with her.

"When Beth and I expressed our eagerness to meet this compassionate woman, he explained she had passed away a few days earlier and that her things had been given to the Helping Hands Ministry, which is why we went there to look for the spoon.

"So do you still have the spoon?" I inquired.

"No," he replied. "After we brought it home, I called my mom to tell her all that had happened. She insisted that I bring the spoon over to her house so that she could see it.

"Mom greeted us at the door with a big smile, but when she saw the spoon she broke down and cried. Apparently the spoon brought back painful memories of our family back when dad was alive. As Dan wrapped his loving arms around mom, she was able to release her grief.

"Afterward, she lovingly held the spoon in her hand as we all gave thanks to God that His ways are better than our own."

"Was that why you left the spoon with your mom?"

"No, I actually left it by mistake. I thought Beth had put it in her purse. When I started to eat cereal the next morning, we realized it was missing. I immediately called mom to make sure it was at her house. She said that it was. She also shared something strange that happened the night before."

"So tell me," I said out of curiosity.

"Mom said it was too late to call when she found I had left the spoon, so she laid it on the dining room table and went to bed. At about midnight, she heard voices downstairs. Rather than wake up Dan, she tiptoed down the steps to investigate, thinking Dan might have just left the TV on.

"As she approached the dining room, she heard a voice saying, 'Is our cousin here?'

'Yes, but don't talk too loudly,' came the reply.

"Thinking intruders were in the house, Mom was about to go wake up Dan when she suddenly heard another voice, only this time she recognized it as being the voice of the bent spoon."

'Forkie, is that really you?' exclaimed the spoon.

'Yes, Cousin. We were just getting ready to surprise you with a welcome home song!'

'Welcome home!' came a symphony of voices.

'We want you to know that we never forgot you,' said one of the teaspoons.

'When you didn't come back that day, we asked the young boy where you were, but he refused to answer. Finally, after several weeks he told us what had happened. We were heartbroken knowing we might not ever see you again. We were even more crushed when he told us he had not only abandoned you, but also abused you to the point of bending your stem. We were so overcome with grief that it took us a long time to forgive him. Finally we realized we had to forgive. We knew you would want us to. Besides, he was as heartbroken as we were. After all, you were his favorite spoon.

'A strange thing happened that night as we each identified with your suffering. Our own stems began to bend, as if we had been allowed to identify with your suffering as a way to express our deep love for you.

'Afterward we chose a name for ourselves that would reflect our new identify,' said one of the forks. 'The name we chose was *Imperfecto*. Although outwardly we are imperfect, in our hearts we are all of one family.'

'Now after all these years,' said Forkie, 'we are finally reunited. If a set of spoons, forks, and knives could cry, a river of joyful tears would have overflowed that night!'

"After listening to the conversation, mom quietly slipped back upstairs. The following evening, she fixed a great meal and invited her many friends to rejoice with her over the return of the discarded spoon and the reunion of the Imperfecto family.

"Each knife, fork, and spoon served its purpose that evening, but it was the tablespoon that had the honor of serving the whole family. Indeed, this was a special celebration, since it was the first evening of Passover.

"After hearing that great story, I knew there was no chance of me having the discarded spoon. As if reading my thoughts, Beth added, 'Mom plans on keeping the spoon and all the other utensils until she passes away, then the whole Imperfecto family will be ours.'

I looked at the couple and said, "I guess I will just have to be content with remembering other ways in which the old woman impacted my life. Indeed, her love for the Misfits and the Discarded has had an impact on many of us."

I suppose the lesson we should learn from all of this is to keep our ears open to "the cry of the misfits and the discarded," I said as I headed out the door.

THE MISFIT CHAIR

The melted plastic was full of excitement, "Surely I will become a work of art with these vivid colors and smooth texture. Maybe I'll be formed into a decorative lamp post to sit at the gate of a mansion, or perhaps I'll be a toy box that will delight the heart of a child."

She watched with growing anticipation as the other liquids were poured into their unique mold. Finally her time came. Joyfully she conformed to the mold set before her. After several days of confinement, the process was finished.

"So what am I?" she wondered as she looked at her odd shape.

Before she had time to find an answer, a man began screwing metal bars beneath her two parts.

"Finished!" he declared with a hearty laugh. The others also joined him in laughter.

"Two colorful leaves joined together to form a chair? That's ridiculous!" said the owner's wife. Don't make any more like that, as they will never sell."

Crushed by the woman's harsh remarks, the oddly-shaped chair sank into depression.

"If only I had been made like the others," the chair said with a heavy sigh.

Finally came the day of the big sale. Each new item was proudly placed on display, except the misfit chair. She was tucked away at the back so as not to be an embarrassment to the owner's wife.

Many people came to the sale, but few noticed the misfit chair. Those that did notice either laughed or ignored her altogether. All the uniquely made pieces were quickly sold—all, that is, except the misfit chair.

"I knew no one would want me," said the chair, as it was overwhelmed by the spirit of hopelessness. Suddenly from out of nowhere, the chair heard a voice saying,

"Don't despair, little chair."

"Who are you?" she replied.

"I'm the one that placed the creative idea in the mind of the one who fashioned you."

"So you are to blame for me being a misfit!" the chair said in anger.

"Yes, I am responsible, but don't give up hope. I have a plan for you."

"Some plan!" complained the chair. "Was it your plan to make me a laughing stock? If so, you succeeded. I'm sorry," the chair quickly added. "I didn't mean to be disrespectful."

As the sale ended, the owner was about to close the gate when a man drove up in a pickup truck. "I just got off work," he said. "Do you have any of your famous works of art left?"

"No," said the owner. "Everything was sold except this multicolored leaf chair."

"How much are you asking for it?"

"You can have it for just five dollars," the owner replied.

"I'll give you three dollars," the truck driver negotiated with a smile.

"OK, it's a deal," the owner said without hesitation.

A sense of belonging enveloped the chair as it was loaded into the back of the man's truck. After reaching the man's house, the chair was unloaded onto the patio. She could hardly contain her excitement when she saw the table and four chairs that were already there.

"Surely, she thought, "they will welcome me into their family, especially since we serve the same purpose."

As the man set the chair down next to the table, one of the chairs spoke up. "Why in the world did he bring that misfit here?" the chair said in disgust.

"You know our owner. He always shows pity on misfits and discards. The old rusty wheelbarrow and the broken pottery in the garden are prime examples. He even gave a special place to that worn-out tea kettle. Since he is compassionate, we should be too," the table responded.

"I guess you are right," said the chair; the other chairs agreed. Although they tried to be polite when the misfit chair was near, they did not hesitate to share their true feelings when she was moved to the other end of the patio.

"I don't know where that misfit got the idea that she could fit in," said one of the chairs. "She doesn't look anything like us."

"Personally, I think she just likes to show off her loud colors, and the fact she only has three legs," said another chair in disgust.

"Let's be fair," said the table. "As I understand it, the man who designed her did so because of a dream he had."

"You mean a nightmare," laughed a chair.

"You need to be careful what you say about the misfit chair," said the table. She may have been sent here to teach us something. After all, the man who designed her is known around the world for his creative masterpieces." Out of respect for the table the chairs quieted down.

Much to the sorrow of many people, near the end of the summer the old man died. Since his wife planned to move in with one of their sons, she auctioned off everything, including the rusty wheelbarrow and the worn out tea kettle. Finally the misfit chair was placed on the block.

"Who will pay five dollars?" the auctioneer called. The crowd grew silent. "Do I hear five?"

"I'll give you two!" a man yelled from the back of the room.

"Two going once, two going twice..."

Suddenly a dignified woman stepped into view, "A thousand dollars!" she shouted.

A hush came over the crowd.

"Did you say one thousand dollars?" the auctioneer asked, as he checked his hearing aid.

"Yes, I did," replied the woman confidently.

The people were amazed, and questioned, "Is she crazy or does the chair indeed have value we cannot see?"

"Going once, going twice—SOLD to the lady for one thousand dollars!" the auctioneer loudly proclaimed.

Bewildered, the chair wondered, "Why would anyone pay such a price for me?"

After the transaction was complete, the woman took the misfit chair to her beautiful home and placed it in the formal living room with its luxurious furnishings.

No longer could the chair keep silent. "Why did you purchase me?" she asked.

"You probably don't remember me," the woman replied, "but right after you were molded, I told my husband that you looked ridiculous, and he should not make any more like you. I thought no more about the matter, until one night I had a dream in which I was transported to heaven. As I stood before our Creator, my whole life was displayed on a giant screen. My heart was broken as I saw how my careless words and harsh treatment had hurt many people. At first, I tried to defend myself by pointing out the things they had said and done to hurt me. However, when the scene showed you, I could make no excuses, for you had done nothing to hurt or offend me. Yet I belittled you to such an extent that my husband threw away the mold from which you were formed. As I continued watching the scene on the giant screen, I saw the hurt and loneliness you suffered because of me. With deepest regret I begged our Creator for forgiveness. I also requested that He let me return to earth to make amends for my sin.

Upon awaking, I began my search for you. I asked my husband if he knew the person who bought you. Although he didn't remember anything about you, I didn't let that stop me. But after searching for months, I finally gave up, as I didn't have a clue as to where you were, until the day of the auction. I just happened to be driving by the auction tent when out of curiosity I decided to stop. As I made my way to the tent, I spotted you on the platform. My heart broke as I saw you being humiliated all over again."

"But why did you bid one thousand dollars?" asked the misfit chair. "You probably could have had me for five dollars."

"My precious chair, the reason is that our Creator showed me your true value!"

"I don't understand," said the chair.

"For years you suffered rejection and abuse, yet you never allowed anger or bitterness to enter your heart. Even when you were mocked, you forgave your tormentors. Therefore, in the heavenly realm, you are of great value, far more than the one thousand dollars I paid."

"But you don't understand! I did get angry in the beginning, and I said some very harsh words about you."

"Did you ask forgiveness?"

"Yes," replied the chair.

"That must have been why our Creator had no record of it. I only wish I had asked His forgiveness sooner," said the woman. Anyway, my precious chair, I am honored to have you here. Welcome to your new home!"

THE ABANDONED PALM BRANCH

"Why are you lying here in the muddy water?" asked the little old lady.

"None of your business," said the palm branch as it turned its face to the water.

"I'm not judging you or trying to be critical because you are here. I'm just concerned," she replied.

"Why should you care? I don't mean anything to you," said the palm branch sharply.

"That's where you are wrong. You do mean something to me, and I do care."

"You are just one of those 'goodie two shoes' that pretends to care just to make a good impression. You just want to make others think you are loving and compassionate."

Although the palm branch's words shot forth like an arrow, the old woman didn't let that stop her.

"I do confess there was a time that your words would have been true, but not anymore. The love and compassion I now have doesn't come from me, it comes from God."

"God, that's a joke! If God cared, why did He let me be cut off from the other branches? As you can see, I am not dry or withered. If I were, I could understand the need to be cut off. But that's not the case. Therefore, I don't believe in God. If there is such a one, he is cruel and unfair. So don't talk to me about God!'

"Who do you think created you?" the old woman asked.

"Certainly not God, or if He did, He must be absentminded, because He forgot all about me."

"I can understand why you say that, but it doesn't make it true," she replied. "I just wish you could bring yourself to the place of acknowledging him and realize he has a purpose for everything that he allows to happen to us." That being said, she headed home.

"Thanks for stopping by," the branch called. "At least you care enough to do that. No one else has been that concerned."

A couple of days later, she returned to find the branch had withered up and all its green color had turned to brown. The branch was also much weaker, yet much to her surprise, he had a smile on his face.

"So how are you?" she asked.

"I'm fine," said the branch.

"How can that be? You look as if you could die any moment."

"That's true, but that no longer bothers me. I have peace, which is all that matters."

"So what brought about this change?"

"After you left, I began talking to the muddy water. It told me it had felt just like me in the beginning. But then God showed her life does have a purpose no matter what circumstances we are in. I asked the water what good she could see in her present circumstances. She said, 'I'm here to give you a drink of water and show you the goodness of God.' The water went on to explain that in a few days the rays from the sun would draw her up to be with the clouds in the sky. Then one day they would all come back to earth again. After she told me that, I asked her what purpose I might have. She said that perhaps my call was to lay down my life to enrich the soil, and that one day the vacant lot might be transformed into a beautiful garden. The thought of that possibility makes me smile. It also helps me to thank God for creating me. As strange as it may sound, I even thanked Him for placing me next to this beautiful mud puddle.

"Thanks for sharing. It makes me happy to know you have such peace. But what do you mean by saying mud puddles are beautiful?"

"Oh but they are. If you look closely you'll see that they reflect the trees and the clouds above them."

"You're right. I never noticed that," said the old woman with a smile.

"By the way," said the branch, "thank you for caring enough to stop by to talk to me. If you had not come by, I might not have realized any of these things. I hope you will forgive me for the harsh things I said to you."

"Of course, I forgive you," said the little old lady.

"I've also asked God to forgive me," said the branch. "I shouldn't have said all those mean things about him. I've asked Him to help my brothers and sisters find the peace I have found. They may still be flourishing on the tree, but some aren't very happy. In fact, they think I'm crazy for telling all those that pass by that God is good. When I was high up in the tree, I couldn't do that. But now that I'm on the ground, I can tell any who will take time to listen."

"Be assured, palm branch, many will hear. And we rejoice with you," said the little old woman as she picked up her walking stick and headed for home.

THE CLOCK THAT WAS STUCK IN TIME

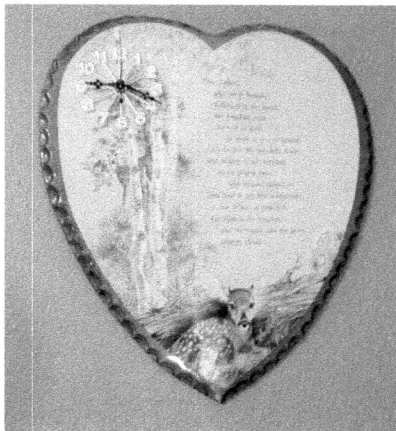

"*I* am no good!" moaned the clock on the wall. "Although I am decorated with the beauty of nature in soft colors of green and brown, and the Lord's Prayer is inscribed upon my heart, I know I'm not what I should be.

"You may ask why I moan and complain. It is because my calling and purpose is to keep time. Yet, if you look closely, you will see that I'm stuck in time. In my far left corner are the face and hands of a clock. I purposely placed them there so as not to distract from the beauty of the nature scene and the words of the holy prayer. But as wonderful as those things are, I know that my main duty is to inform people of the time.

"In this, I am a failure because my hands are stuck. I have no strength or power to move them. I don't know if this is an internal or external problem, I only know I can't function properly.

"I am about to be hauled off to the dump or discarded at the thrift shop, along with the other misfits and undesirables. I begged the woman who has me in her home not to do this. However, she won't listen to my pleas for mercy. Any day now I will be sent away in disgrace."

"Not so! I have been sent here to help you," said the little old woman.

"Who are you to think you can help?" asked the clock.

"It's not about who I am, it's about my purpose—to respond to the cry of the misfits and the discarded."

"Do you actually think there is hope for me?" asked the clock.

"Of course, there is hope. You are very special," she responded.

"How can you say I'm special? You don't know anything about me."

"No. But your Creator knows, and He is the One who sent me. So if He says you are special, then I believe it."

"Hummm, I don't think He really knows me. Otherwise He wouldn't say I was special," he replied.

"Why would you say that?" the old woman asked.

"Because I doubt he knows all the places I've been and the things I have done. You see, this is not the first woman who has taken me in. There have been others who were drawn to me because of my outward appearance. However, I let them down by not keeping the proper time. So sooner or later I get discarded. Oh there were some who liked me enough to keep me around because of my outward appearance, but that's not what I want. My deepest desire is to fulfill my true calling. But as long as I am stuck in time, I can't do that."

"So tell me," said the little old woman, "what is hindering you from going forward?"

"I think it is related to a traumatic experience I had when I was young."

"What do you mean?" she asked. "Is it something you can share with me?"

"Perhaps, but I'm not sure you will understand," said the clock.

"Why not give me a try?"

Over the course of the next few weeks, the clock shared many grievous things that had happened in his past. With great love and sympathy, the old woman listened. She even tried to comfort the clock with an occasional hug. The more the clock shared, the more the little old lady grew to love him. She so enjoyed his company that she didn't care if he couldn't keep time. She just wanted to help him. The clock also liked being with the old woman as she encouraged him to fulfill his purpose in life. She even replaced his battery in the hope of jump-starting him into fulfilling his purpose. But even that didn't help.

As time went on, however, the clock began to back off from the little old woman as he felt she was trying to control him. Finally, he confronted her about the matter. She wept as she realized she had forgotten the purpose for which the Creator had sent her, which was to help him fulfill his destiny. After repenting for her failure, she withdrew from the clock. Although this was not easy, she knew it was necessary not only for his sake but also for hers. Indeed she had allowed him to consume too much of her time and attention.

One day, as she was sharing these things with her friend, her friend said, "Let me see if I can fix the clock by putting in new batteries."

"That's not the problem," said the little old woman. "I've already tried that but it didn't work."

"No wonder," said her friend. "You put the batteries in backwards." Carefully her friend placed the batteries in correctly, and within moments, the clock began to tick properly.

"I'm free! I'm free!" He exclaimed with great joy. "I can finally go forward as I am no longer stuck in memories of the past!"

Indeed the clock did go forth in all that the Creator intended for him. No longer did it matter to him where he was or who was with him. His delight was in telling everyone that "It was time to seek the Lord!" The news of this delighted the little old woman! Perhaps, in some small way, she might have helped him after all, even if only through her prayers.

THE OUTDATED COMPUTER

"You can't do this to me!" the computer screamed. "I've been faithful to you for years. You can't just toss me out."

"I've tried to tell you, this is nothing personal. You are just outdated. When I first bought you, you served me well. I even boasted to all my friends about how well you worked and what a great help you were to me," the man explained.

"I know, so why have you suddenly decided to get rid of me?" the computer asked, trying to hide feelings of hurt and rejection.

"You don't understand. I can't just keep you around for sentimental reasons. The bottom line is, you are outdated. I need technology that is faster and more efficient."

"I agree I'm not as fast as I was when you first got me, but that's because you loaded me down with so much junk. If you remove some of that, I'll prove I can be faster than ever."

"You still don't understand. A more updated computer can handle ten times more than you on your fastest day. Plus it can correct mistakes I make. Besides that, your keys have been getting stuck lately. And remember, you have crashed on me a couple of times this past week."

"What do you expect? I'm not as young as I use to be," the computer replied.

"That's exactly my point. I need to replace you. However, I can let you hang around for a few weeks while I get adjusted to my new computer."

Overwhelmed by hurt and rejection, the computer froze up completely.

"See! That's what I'm talking about. You freeze up for no apparent reason. I'm sick and tired of you doing that!" Angrily the man grabbed up the computer and headed to the nearest dumpster.

"I thought you said you would at least give me a few more weeks," said the computer as it saw the direction they were headed.

"I would have, but with your nasty attitude, who needs you! I've got enough problems without having to deal with an incompatible computer."

"But couldn't you at least give me to somebody that can't afford a new computer, or maybe just let a child use me as a learning toy?"

"I might have considered such a thing had you not been so defiant, but now I'm just going to throw you in the dumpster."

Although the computer was speechless, negative thoughts were running rampantly in his mind. "What a fool I was to think I was special to my owner. Apparently I was just a piece of equipment to him—just something to be used, abused, and now discarded. All right, let him throw me in the dumpster. I don't care! I'm just sorry I wasted all those years trying to serve him. Nothing matters to me anymore. I don't want to go on functioning for him or anyone else, for that matter." Depression set in, and the computer became silent.

As the owner neared the dumpster, his anger began to subside as a tinge of guilt surfaced. Instead of hurling the computer into the dumpster as he intended, he loosened his grip and dropped it to the ground. It hit the dirt with a crash, breaking off several pieces which flew in different directions. Although the owner felt a slight bit of guilt, he just turned and walked away.

"Oh GOD, at least I thought you cared about me, but apparently you don't. If you did, you wouldn't leave me here," cried the discarded computer as it lay broken on the ground.

"Wait," whispered the voice of a gentle breeze as it passed by.

"Wait for what?" the computer cried. "There's no possible hope for me."

As the computer continued to lie on the ground for the next several days, he tried to forget the message given by the gentle breeze. Yet for some reason he couldn't delete it from his memory.

Early one morning, a little old woman walking her dog noticed the discarded computer. "You poor thing, why are you here?" she asked.

"I'm just old and useless," replied the computer.

"I don't agree with that! I'll bet if those broken parts were fixed, you would still have a lot of life in you," she said with a smile.

"I wish that were true, but I don't think it is. Besides, even if that was possible, who would care enough to go to the trouble and expense to fix me?"

"I would," said the little old woman as she gently picked up it off the ground.

"Are you really serious?" the discarded computer asked as a spark of hope ignited within him.

"Of course, I'm serious. I have a friend who fixes old computers. I'll have him check out your problems. If it doesn't cost too much, we will get you fixed."

"Why would you do such a thing for me?" the computer asked.

"Because when I was broken and in disrepair, someone took the time to help me," she said with a smile.

The old woman took the discarded computer to her friend's shop for repair. "So what do you think, Dave? Is there any hope for this computer?" she asked as she placed it on the counter.

"We'll soon see," he said as he began taking it apart. "Hummm, it does need several parts. But other than that, it looks like it's in fairly good shape."

"Good. Then what will the repairs cost?" she asked.

"Don't you have a birthday coming up soon?" he asked.

"Yes, I'll be 83 years old," she said with a sheepish grin.

"Good, then these repairs will be my birthday gift to you," Dave said with a smile.

After repairing and refurbishing the computer, Dave placed it in the window of his shop while waiting for the old woman to pick it up. Just then, the original owner of the computer came by the shop.

"That computer you just put in the window looks exactly like the one I use to have," the man said as he hurried inside. "I would be interested in buying it."

"Sorry, it's not for sale," Dave replied. "It belongs to a little old woman."

"Do you suppose she would sell it to me?" he asked.

"Here she comes. You can ask her yourself," Dave replied.

"What makes you interested in buying this particular computer?" the old woman asked.

"It reminds me of the one I use to have. It was such a reliable computer, but as it began to get old, I had a few problems with it. Then foolishly I decided to discard it and get a more updated model."

"What did you do with your old computer?" she inquired.

"I'm embarrassed to say that in a fit of anger I threw it on the ground near the trash dump. I thought I could just forget about it, but I couldn't. I lay awake that night thinking about how harshly I had treated my computer. Finally, I decided to go to the dump and retrieve it, but by that time it was gone. I know it was just a computer, but somehow it felt as if I had lost a trusted friend. That's why when I saw the computer in the window and it looked like my old one, I wanted to buy it."

"If I should let you have this one, will you discard it like you did your old one?" she asked.

"No! I will not be so foolish again. I will use it to teach my grandson how to use computers. I'll also teach him to be patient if it freezes up occasionally or doesn't work as fast as newer models."

After hearing the man's story, the old woman turned to the computer and said, "You have heard what he said. Are you willing to go with him?"

Although the computer knew he had every right to hold a grudge against his former owner, he just couldn't do it. So he nodded his approval to the old woman.

As she handed the computer to the man, she declared, "This is your old computer."

"Really?" he exclaimed with great joy. "I'm so happy! How much do I owe you for it?"

"No charge. Just don't let something like this happen again," she said very sternly.

"I won't!" said the man as he lovingly clutched the computer and headed out the door.

THE DISCARDED
FASHION BOOT

"*P*ardon us," said the pair of fashion boots, as the young girl took them to the cash register to make her purchase.

"Why did she choose those boots instead of us?" asked an ordinary pair of boots. "We are far more comfortable."

"The young girl wasn't looking for comfort," said another. "She was looking for style. So, of course, she chose the most popular boots on the market," said a pair of kind-hearted boots.

"She'll live to regret it," said another.

"Don't say that! We need to pray that they will make the adjustment."

"That's a joke. That young girl will never have the patience to do all the lacing up that the stylish boots require."

"It's not our place to judge what anyone will do or not do," continued the kind-hearted boots.

"I'm tired of you always giving us a lecture about what we say or do, Miss Holier-Than-Thou."

"I agree," chimed in a pair of loafers. "We have a right to our opinion just as much as she does."

"I apologize for coming on so strong. I just know that what we sow is what we reap."

"If that's true," said the loafers, "then Miss Fashion Boots is in for a lot of trouble. She has criticized every boot in the store, plus many of the other shoes."

"That's why no one likes her," said the simple boots.

"Personally, I'm glad she's gone! She and that young girl with the arrogant attitude should make a good match."

"Don't say I didn't warn all of you if your own words come back to haunt you."

Meanwhile, the young girl and her fashion boots were having difficulty making adjustment. "You stupid boot why are you making it so hard for me to slip my foot inside?"

"I'm not making it hard for you. You just have to unlace me, at least part of the way."

"I don't have time to unlace you. When I bought you I thought I could just loosen a few strings, not have to totally undo them."

"I'm sorry, that's just not the case," said one of the fashion boots.

"You should be! You lured me into buying you with your sleek look. I've a good mind to throw you across the room!" said the girl. But instead she stormed out of the room. The boot she had threatened began to sob.

The other boot was furious. "She had no right to say all those hateful things to us."

"She didn't mean it. Something must be hurting her," said the kind-hearted boot.

"You are beginning to sound just like that pair of holier-than-thou boots that was in the store. Besides, I don't know how you could take up for the girl. You were the one she threatened to throw across the room. The truth of the matter is that girl is just hateful and mean."

"I understand what you are saying, as it does appear that way on the surface. However, I believe it's all just to cover up her own pain."

"Say what you will, but she is not going to talk to me or you that way. Sooner or later I'm going to find a way to get even."

Sure enough the boot gave the girl a hard time by rubbing a big blister on her toe. However, the other boot remained kind and thoughtful and never did anything to hurt the girl.

One day after causing the young girl an extreme amount of pain, she threw the boot across the room. Although the boot slammed into the wall, it remained defiant as always.

The next day, the young girl took the boot to the dumpster. "It's with great pleasure I throw you in," said the girl to the defiant boot.

She then looked at the other boot. "I take no pleasure in getting rid of you," she said. "But one boot without the other will be of no help to me." She laid the boot on the ground outside the dumpster. "Perhaps you will find a friend among the other discards," she said.

"Wait!" cried the boot. "Will you do me one favor before you go? Tell me why you have been so harsh and angry?"

"Do you really want to know?" asked the girl as tears came to her eyes.

"Yes, I do," said the boot.

"When I was born," said the girl, "both my parents loved me dearly, especially my dad. He would hold me close when I was hurting and rock me when I couldn't sleep. My mom also loved me, but in a different sort of way. She always made sure I was appropriately dressed and that I had friends to play with. However, I was never quite sure if she did these things because she loved me or she just felt it was the proper thing to do.

"Unlike my dad, she came from a rich family that was held in high regard in the community. Therefore, she would not do anything to jeopardize her reputation or that of her mother's family.

"That's the part that caused so many problems between her and my dad. He believed in being real, which was what I loved most about my dad. If he said he loved me, I knew it came from his heart.

"Mom would also say she loved me, especially when her friends were around, but I was never quite sure if she meant it or was just trying to impress them as to what a good mother she was.

"When I was about five years old, my dad left us. He never even said goodbye. I can't begin to tell you what pain that brought to me. When I asked my mom why he left, she just said he had his reasons. Mom knew how badly I was hurting, so she tried to make up for the loss by giving me everything I wanted—everything, that is, except love and affection. She really did not know how to show affection because she had never received any when she was growing up.

So instead of being like my dad, I grew up as a spoiled brat that had to have my way about everything. Of course, I lost many of my friends because of this, all except Julie. She is the only one that ever loved me no matter how hateful I would be."

"I'm glad you at least have her as a friend," said the boot.

"I'm glad too. Anyway, I'm sorry to leave you here, but I don't know anything else I can do."

"It's OK. I'll make some new friends," said the boot.

"I'm sure you will. The other discards can't help but love you, as you have such a compassionate heart," the young girl said as she turned and walked away.

That night the boot in the dumpster talked to the one that was left outside on the ground. "I overheard your conversation with the young girl today. I must admit, you have a lot more compassion than I do. But I still say the girl was wrong. No matter what her life has been like, she had no right to treat us like she did."

"Could the same be said of you?" asked the other boot.

"Oh but I had a reason…," her voice trailed off as she realized there was no excuse for her behavior. I wish I could see the girl again so that I could ask her forgiveness before being hauled off to the dump. Just in case you don't get taken away with the rest of us, would you please let her know that I am sorry for the way I acted."

"If I happen to see her, I'll share what you said."

"Thanks. I want you to know that I'm also going to get things right with my Creator."

"Good, that's a wise thing for each of us to do," said the boot on the ground.

When the dump truck came by the next day, the men emptied the dumpster, but failed to pick up the boot on the ground. A few hours later, the young girl came back, only this time, she was with her friend Julie.

"After I left you, my friend Julie came to visit. I told her how you had blessed and encouraged me. She suggested that we come and pick you up if you were still here."

"Why would you want to do that?" asked the boot.

"You have a purpose," Julie said with a smile. "Your love and compassion will be an inspiration to others."

"I'm not sure I can be an inspiration to anyone as I'm still grieving for the other boot that was taken to the dump this morning. By the way, she did want me to tell you she was sorry for the way she treated you."

"I'm also sorry," said the girl. "Perhaps I was a bit too hasty in discarding her. Hopefully I've learned my lesson so that I will never do something like that again."

"I think we have all learned a lot of lessons."

"I don't mean to interrupt," Julie said "I would like to get a picture of you lying on the ground."

"I don't understand why you want a picture of me. I'm nothing but a tattered old boot that doesn't even have a mate."

"That may be true, but you have a testimony that needs to be shared with others."

"If you think what I have gone through will help others, then feel free to share it."

"I agree," said the young girl. "By the way, I would love to take you to meet a little old woman that loves to collect misfits and discards. I'm sure she will be delighted to let you stay with her for the rest of your days," Julie said with a smile.

THE BROKEN
POTTERY

"*H*ow beautiful," said the man as he designed the clay pot.

"Why did you say that?" asked his young son. It looks no different from the others.

"My son, you only see it as it is now. I see its future."

"You mean somebody wealthy will buy it and give it a place of importance?"

"No, I foresee it as a pot that will be moved from place to place. In the process, it will be dropped, and a piece will be broken off."

"I don't understand," said the young boy. "How can you say it's beautiful if it's going to end up a broken piece of clay? Doesn't that mean it will be thrown in the trash dump?"

"Yes, that's exactly where it would end up were it not for the old man who loves to collect misfits and discards."

"Is this the man that bought the misfit chair?"

"Yes, he is the one."

"Why does he like such things? It doesn't make sense?"

"It would if you knew the whole story," said his father.

"So tell me, what is his story?"

"He had a defect when he was born. Because his parents were too poor to afford the expense of medical treatment that was needed, the doctor advised them to give him up at birth. His parents thought about what the doctor had said, but after much prayer, they decided to keep their baby, no matter the cost. It was a great struggle for them financially. However, they willingly sacrificed many things for his sake.

The young boy was very happy when the time came to enroll him in school. His hope was to make many new friends, especially since he had no brothers or sisters. But things didn't work out the way he had hoped. Some of his classmates made fun of him because of the way he had to drag his one leg. He also had no control over his left arm, and his speech was slurred. The children viewed him as a misfit and purposely avoided him. There was only one girl in the class who would talk to him. The others mocked her for befriending him, but she didn't let that bother her, because at birth she too had known rejection. You may have read about her in the paper years ago. She was the baby abandoned in a dumpster. A man passing by heard her cry and saved her life. This girl continued to be the boy's friend through the years and eventually they grew up and got married."

"So did the young boy's condition ever get better?" the boy asked.

"No, he was not healed of his condition. But he and his wife were so filled with compassion for others that they committed their lives to helping those who were rejected and discarded. One way they did this was by collecting things like a rusty old wheelbarrow and a discarded tea pot."

"Is the old man's wife the one that collects things from the dump?" asked the young boy.

"Yes, and they will also take care of this pot when it is broken."

"But how can such things help people with disabilities?" the boy asked.

"The man and his wife use these items to show that those who are disabled can still be used mightily by their Creator."

"So how will this clay pot be used?"

"Thanks for asking," said the clay pot. "I've been eavesdropping on your conversation. And I hope you don't mind if I answer his question."

The boy's father smiled and nodded his approval.

"To be quite frank," continued the broken pot, "I was upset when your father first started prophesying such a doom and gloom future for me, but now I'm encouraged to know I will ultimately serve a purpose such as this. I just want to know how I'm to do it."

The man replied, "You don't have to do anything accept yield to your Creator's plans and purposes. However, in your particular case, I see you gently holding a little vine that has been cut off from its mother. You will nurture it and surround it with love so that it can grow strong and beautiful. When those that have disabilities see that you are not bemoaning the fact that you are broken or holding unforgiveness toward the one that dropped you, and that your life still has purpose, they will be encouraged to follow your example."

"Wow! I love that. Why can't I just go directly to the person who is going to drop me? The sooner the better, I always say," replied the clay pot.

"Sorry, that's not how it works," answered the man. "You must endure the process, which may require many years of hardship. If you were dropped right now, you would fall apart completely because you are still brittle. But as time goes on and you learn to serve others, you will become stronger. The reason I told you what would finally happen was so that you would endure to the end."

"Yes, and I will endure!" exclaimed the clay pot. "By the help of my Creator I will learn to rejoice in every situation, knowing that all things work together for good to those who love Him. Thank you for giving me such hope for the future!" said the pot with a big smile.

THE LEAVES THAT
REFUSED TO FALL

"You're right," said the little old woman to her friend. "Watching leaves change from green to bright orange is a spectacular event. Indeed their last dance in the autumn wind draws the attention and admiration of many. However, it's not those that display their glory that catch my attention the most. I'm inspired by the few leaves that cling to the branch in spite of knowing that cold, dark days are ahead.

"Strong winds, rain, and snow will try to loosen their grip, yet those leaves will continue to hold on with determination. Even though nourishment will not be provided and they will dry up and become old and ugly, they will still hang on because they know their purpose has not yet been fulfilled.

"Their ultimate goal is to hold on until the bright green leaves bud, taking their place in the spring. When this happens, they will gladly fall to the ground. In the meantime, few people will notice these leaves or give them any recognition. Yet those who do recognize their sacrifice will be helped and encouraged to fulfill their own destiny.

"Unfortunately not all leaves that begin this difficult task will be able to endure," said the old woman. "But they will still be blessed for at least trying. A great reward awaits those that do make it though—a reward not in this life but in the life to come. They will hear the words of their Creator, 'Well done, my good and faithful servant.'

"When these faithful leaves fall to the ground, the power and virtue they had will be used to enrich the soil for those that come after them. This will give the persevering leaves much joy and satisfaction!

"I will enjoy the beauty of the falling leaves as my friend does. However, I will not forget the faithful few that shall fulfill their destiny in a different way," said the old woman as she concluded her story.

About the Author

From the age of 7 to 11, Aliza spent most of her time in and out of the hospital due to a bone infection in her leg that eventually caused her leg to be deformed. This began her personal journey of feeling like a misfit.

Since the hospital had no special place for children, Aliza was placed in a ward with sick babies who cried day and night. On one occasion, she noticed a nurse being mean to one of the babies. When Aliza shared this with her mother, the nurse happened to overhear the conversation. Later, she threatened Aliza and had her moved to an adult ward with about 30 men and women. Although the patients were nice to Aliza, she still felt like a lonely little misfit.

Visiting hours were especially difficult, as Aliza's parents lived 50 miles away. Since gas was rationed, they were only able to visit her once every two weeks. While others enjoyed the company of family and friends, Aliza moved her wheelchair to a quiet spot in the hall and cried till there were no tears left. During one of these cries, Aliza remembered a popular song that included the words *"for every bit of sadness, there will be a little bit of gladness."* Later she could testify to the truth of these words ...

After missing three years of school, Aliza was finally able to go back to school with the use of crutches. With great anticipation, she entered the third grade. Although the children were several years younger than her, Aliza was still glad to be with them. However, her joy was short-lived, as she was mocked, spit upon and even called a devil. Like a sharp knife, the pain of this rejection was buried deep in Aliza's heart for many years. One day after 40 years of carrying this hurt, she cried and shared these memories with a close friend. The Lord suddenly spoke to Aliza's heart and said, "How long will you go on hurting? Forgive and the hurt will go away." Receiving this word from the Lord, Aliza cried out the name of the person that had hurt her the most and said, "Ruby, I forgive you!" Instantly, the knife of rejection was removed from her heart.

God used these experiences to teach Aliza some of her most valuable lessons. Indeed, it was out of these experiences that *The Cry of the Misfits and the Discarded* was birthed.

Author website: www.israelmyfriend.com

www.ingramcontent.com/pod-product-compliance
Lightning Source LLC
Chambersburg PA
CBHW060532030426
42337CB00021B/4224